la philosophie de

CANTONA

la philosophie de

CANTONA

A bilingual celebration of Art and Beauty
through the words of Eric Cantona

edited by

MICHAEL ROBINSON

Translations by Sophie Nusslé

Ringpull

Published by Ringpull Press Ltd, 1995

Ringpull Press Limited
Queensway House
London Road South
Poynton
Greater Manchester
SK12 1NJ

A CIP catalogue record for this book is available from the British Library

ISBN 1 89805139 9

Designed by **Joe Magee**

Printed in England by Clays Limited, St Ives plc.

la philosophie de
CANTONA

This book is respectfully
dedicated to the genius
of Eric Cantona

INTRODUCTION

When Eric Cantona came to England in January 1992 he made the most significant northward Channel crossing since that of William the Conqueror in the long forgotten season of 1066/67. For not only did he dazzle the footballing fraternity – he also raised eyebrows in intellectual circles. Fans of both the long ball and the astute aphorism rose in unison to applaud the audacious skills and flamboyant style of a man whose influence is now all pervasive.

Albert Camus was the first of the footballing

philosophers. A French-Algerian goalkeeper, he pondered long and hard between the sticks, and later produced such existential standards as *The Plague* and *The Rebel*. After the death of Camus in 1960 the twin disciplines of football and philosophy drifted apart. The likes of Law, Best and Charlton set the stadium ablaze, but made precious few assaults on the greater complexities. Similarly, while Jean-Paul Sartre and Jacques Derrida were never short of an insight or a deconstruction, they fell down badly in terms of dribbling and passing.

At which point we welcome Eric Cantona, footballing philosopher of the modern age; a man whose vision encompasses both the shortest route to goal and the more awkward path to meaningful self-knowledge.

This time, with so accessible an example, surely others will follow. In the future every wing-back worth his salt will pontificate openly on the higher purpose, while earnest undergraduates will pop outside after lectures to work on their ball skills.

To date the world of Cultural Studies has not done justice to the Cantona phenomenon. His words have been scattered like beaten defenders, in an article here and an interview there, depriving the reader of an essential overview. Now, at last, the balance is redressed. Collected here, in the raw, are the thoughts of Eric

Cantona. Recurrent themes emerge - forming the basis of *la philosophie* - but there is nothing so shallow as a political creed. Is Eric Cantona a left-winger? No - that's Ryan Giggs.

This volume is designed to be fan-friendly - you can fit it in your pocket and take it to the game. In my dreams I see forty thousand people packed inside a stadium, rising as one in spontaneous *hommage* to a man in a red shirt. Above their heads they hold this little red book, and from their lips bursts the name of Eric Cantona - a fitting tribute to a man who not only knows the score but frequently figures on the scoresheet.

dreams of
CHILDHOOD

Le petit Cantona emerged from the tunnel in the hilly regions outside Marseille in Southern France. He often looks back to those days of youthful exuberance, recalling unrestricted freedom and games without referees. A footballing prodigy, he was whisked away from home to join his first club at the age of fifteen. But those who study his words will soon realise that he never really left that early idyll; he merely packed it with his boots and took it with him.

Quand on a trois ans,

quatre ans, cinq ans, quand on joue dans la
rue avec nos copains, quand on allait
jouer le dimanche matin, et on se levait très
tard dans la nuit pour voir si tout était
en place et si on ne nous avait pas volé les
chaussures, ça c'est vraiment la passion.

When you are three,

four, five years old, and you play football
in the street with your pals, when you
play on a Sunday morning, and you wake up
in the middle of the night to check that
everything is in its place and that no one has
stolen your football boots: that's passion.

En vérité,

il n'y a pas plus belle enfance que celle qui
hésite entre le sport et l'imaginaire.

Il faut admettre

que le football du grand air nous a donné
un formidable besoin de liberté.

In truth,

there is no finer childhood than that which is
balanced between sport and the imaginary.

It has to be said

that playing football in the streets gave
us a tremendous need for freedom.

Je suis un fils de riches!

Mais chez nous, la richesse n'a jamais
été celle de l'argent, du luxe ou bien de la
dépense. Franchement, je souhaite
à tous les enfants qui me demandent des
autographes d'avoir, pour débuter
dans la vie, les mêmes valeurs que celles qui
m'ont été transmises par ma famille,
sur les hauteurs de Marseille.

I am a son of rich people!

But in our house riches have
never meant money or luxury or spending.
Frankly, I wish that all those children
who ask for my autograph could
have, at the start of their lives, the same
values which were passed on to
me by my family in the hills of Marseille.

Si tu n'est pas

spontané, tu ne peux pas réussir.

Without

spontaneity, you can't succeed.

Les enfants

vont où se trouvent la sincérité et
l'authenticité. Dans ma façon de travailler,
de faire mon métier, je ne les trahis pas,
ils le savent. Je ne trouve pas que ce soit
mieux de leur apprendre à renier
leurs émotions au profit de l'ordre établi.

Vieillir

ne signifie pas qu'il faille trahir
sa jeunesse, ses excès.

Children

are drawn to sincerity and authenticity.
The way I work and pursue my career,
I don't betray them and they know it.
I don't see any good in teaching them to
deny their own emotions for the benefit of
the established order.

Growing old

doesn't mean that you have to betray
your youth, your excesses.

Le monde

des enfants, voilà bien ce que je n'aurais
jamais dû quitter.

I wish

I had never had to
grow up.

the art of
FOOTBALL

Some see football as little more than a recreational facility for louts. Wiser ones recognise that within its turbulence and euphoria lies a vivid metaphor for the human condition. Had Kenny Rogers been born in an English footballing town, then the words to his famous song *The Gambler* might have gone a little differently: *You've got to know when to play it short, learn when to knock it long...*

Eric Cantona also draws parallels between the great game of football and the greater game of life. He does not, however, front a Country & Western band.

Le football

c'est le plus beau des arts.

Football

is the most beautiful of the arts.

Un bon but

est un but important

et un beau but.

A good goal

is one which is

important and beautiful.

Il faudra bien

qu'un jour ceux qui bâtissent le football comprennent qu'il n'y a point de salut sans artiste. Bien sûr qu'il faut gagner. Mais il faut admettre la défaite pour que le football soit encore source d'émotion.

One day

those who make football will have to
understand that there is no salvation
without the artist. Of course you have
to win. But you also have to admit
defeat so that football can again be
a source of emotion.

Le football

est peut-être le dernier spectacle susceptible de créer une relation sociale libre et intense. Personne n'est obligé de venir au stade. Personne n'est tenu de chanter.

Platini, il a une idée

que j'ai trouvée était une bonne idée. Il veut interdire le 'tackle' par derrière. Voilà une bonne chose. Mais il y a beaucoup de joueurs, il faut qu'ils fassent vite leurs valises.

Football

is perhaps the last spectacle which is
able to create an open and intense social
relationship. Nobody is forced to come to the
stadium. Nobody is made to sing.

Platini had an idea

which I thought was good. He wanted to
ban the tackle from behind. That's a good
thing, but many players would have to pack
their bags pretty quick.

Sans amitié

dans le football, tu ne peux pas aller
très loin...même si tu es doué.

Without friendship

in football you can't go very far...

even if you are gifted.

Nous les footballeurs,
on a de la chance. On est en bonne santé, on
fait un jeu, on est en plein air, on gagne de
l'argent, on gagne des trophées. Mais en
même temps il ne faut pas perdre conscience
de ce qui se passe autour de nous.

Si on ne gagnait pas
ce qu'on gagne, si je ne gagnais rien du
tout, si je ne gagnais pas un franc, je
jouerais quand même au football.

We footballers

are lucky. We are healthy, we play a game,
we work outdoors, and we earn money and
win trophies. All the same we must never
lose our sense of what's going on around us.

Even if we did not earn

as much as we do, if I earned nothing,
if I never made a penny playing the game,
I would still play football.

N'oublions pas

que le lieu de vérité pour l'athlète est,

et restera, le stade.

L'image du football

d'aujourd'hui, c'est de la sueur et des muscles

hypertrophiés par l'effort. Moi je rêve

de légèreté, d'harmonie, de plaisir. Je suis à

la recherche d'une symphonie. Mais

la musique du football, de nos jours, c'est

seulement du hard rock.

Let us not forget

that the place of truth for an athlete is,

and will always be, the stadium.

The image of football

today is of sweat and of muscles strained

through effort. But I dream of lightness,

harmony and pleasure. I am looking for

a symphony, but the music of football these

days is nothing but heavy metal.

Lorsqu'on a fait très jeune

l'apprentissage de la beauté, on y renonce
difficilement. Un bon footballeur est
forcément un beau joueur.

When you are taught

beauty at an early age, it is very difficult
to give it up. A good footballer is by nature
a beautiful footballer.

WANDERLUST

Eric Cantona turned up his collar for five different French clubs, frequently moving on following a series of sometimes violent bust-ups with team-mates, referees, and club and league officials, most memorably branding his international team manager of the time as something approximating to a 'sack of manure'. How many times in the last twenty years have those of us who despair of our own national team longed for a squad member of similar eloquence?

C'est au moment

d'ouvrir la porte que l'on mesure son
attachement à un lieu, à une maison,
à sa famille.

It is only at the moment

of leaving that you realise how much you

are attached to a place, to a house,

or to your family.

Le décor de ma vie

prouve à lui seul que je suis désormais
de passage, quel que soit le club, la ville
qui m'accueillent. J'ai trop souffert
de vouloir m'attacher.

Whatever club

I'm playing for, wherever I'm living, I never think of myself as a permanent fixture. I've been hurt too many times to ever let myself feel that I belong.

D'être passé

par beaucoup d'endroits, c'est
important. Moi, j'ai voyagé, j'ai vu des
gens, et ça, c'est important. C'est
important pour toi, et c'est important pour
la relation avec les autres.

Les imbéciles

demeurent persuadés qu'un footballeur
va d'abord où se trouve l'argent. S'ils ont
envie de ne pas mourir idiots, qu'ils
sachent que d'autres paramètres font
partie des négociations.

It's important

to have been places. I have travelled.
I've seen many people, and that's
important. It's important for yourself,
and for your relationship with others.

Fools

are convinced that a footballer goes only
where the money is. If they don't want to
die ignorant, they should realise that
there are other issues which form
part of the negotiations.

Je me dis

que je suis de passage...

I say to myself:

I'm just passing through...

ENGLAND

Outlawed in France, Eric Cantona passed through Customs and entered English culture. He cut a pop record, and everyone knows that the French can't do that. All were impressed by his endurance and adaptability. He even survived a spell with Leeds United. Nowadays we regard him as an honorary *rosbif*. Most impressive of all, he frequently denounces the crab-like motion and cheap theatrics of the Continental playing fields, championing instead the true blood and thunder of our own national pastime.

Je ne jouerai plus

en Équipe de France tant qu'Henri Michel
sera là. Ne me parlez plus de lui.
Il faudra choisir entre Michel et moi.
Je souhaite qu'on s'aperçoive qu'il est un
des sélectionneurs les plus incompétents
du football mondial. Je ne suis pas loin de
penser qu'il est un sac à merde.

On m'a dit

il y a un truc en Angleterre. J'ai dit j'aimerais
bien y partir parce-que je crois que les
gens me correspondent, je crois que c'est un
football joué comme il faut. Surtout
les gens. Surtout le façon de vivre. Et je ne
crois pas m'être trompé.

I will never play for France

again whilst Henri Michel is there. Don't talk to me about him. They must choose between Michel and myself. I want people to realise that he is one of the most incompetent managers in world football. I am not far from thinking that he is a shitbag.

I was told

there's something about England. I said I'd like to go there because I thought the people would suit me, and football is played there as it should be. Especially the people. And the lifestyle. That's what I thought and I don't think I was wrong.

Mon cœur et mes jambes

étaient faits pour s'entendre avec le
football britannique.

My heart and my legs

were made to play British football.

On dit que

les Anglais sont arrogants.

Je dis qu'ils ont la justification.

People say

the English are arrogant.

I say they have reason.

Les spectateurs

sont très proches. Ça donne
envie de jouer au football.

The spectators

are very close. That makes
you want to play football.

J'aime la vitesse

du jeu ici. Jouer en allant d'un bout à l'autre
du terrain, garder le rythme constamment.
Il y a de la beauté dans le jeu ici, parce que
la spontanéité, c'est beau.

Ce qui me plaît le plus,

c'est quand une equipe joue pour gagner,
non pas pour perdre. Ça devient de plus
en plus rare, ailleurs qu'en Angleterre.
Ici, on voit des buts.

I love the speed

of the game here. Playing from goal to goal, keeping the momentum going at all times. There's beauty in the game here. The spontaneity is beautiful.

What pleases me most

is when a team plays to win rather than to lose. That's becoming more and more rare outside England. Here you see goals.

Le foot a toujours

déchaîné les passions. Tatouages sur les bras, larmes versées lors du départ d'une vedette, l'émotion est partout.

D'Oldham à Chelsea

et de Liverpool à Luton, mon cœur s'est mis à battre au rythme des fans.

Football has always

unleashed great passions here. Tattoos on
the arm, tears spilt when a star player leaves
— emotion is everywhere.

From Oldham to Chelsea

and from Liverpool to Luton, my heart beats
to the rhythm of the fans.

manchester
UNITED

When Manchester United signed Cantona in
November 1992 some people said it was a risky
move. These are the same people who bought
Betamax videos and thought lottery tickets
wouldn't sell. In truth United and Cantona go
together like fish and chips, like Abbot and
Costello. And with United Cantona has realised
his dream: a club big enough to harness both his
talent and personality. And United too have found
theirs: a player with the flair and panache to
match the legends of old.

Tout que je savais

de Manchester United, c'était qu'à ce
moment là ils recherchaient un attaquant...

Il y a dans une carrière

— appelez cela du nom qu'il vous plaira,
déclic, étape, révélation, peu importe
— une journeé magique à coup sûr.

All I knew

about Manchester United was that they
were looking for a striker...

There is in every career

— call it by whatever name you please:
a trigger point, a stage, a revelation,
it doesn't really matter - a magic day.

Quand je les vois,

qu'ils me touchent, quand ils me parlent
à voix basse, ces gosses des quartiers de
Manchester, je voudrais qu'ils repartent
heureux et convaincus d'avoir rencontré
un joueur qui leur ressemble plus qu'ils
ne le croient.

When I see them,

these boys from Manchester, when they touch me, when they speak to me in hushed voices, I want them to go away happy and convinced that they have met a player who is more like them than they know.

Je suis amoureux de

Manchester United. C'est comme trouver une femme qui m'a donné un mariage parfait.

I am in love with

Manchester United. It is like finding a wife who has given me the perfect marriage.

J'aime la verité,

le respect pour les autres, la compassion et la comprehension. J'ai trouvé ces qualités à Manchester United.

Je me sens proche

de cette jeunesse insolente et vivante. Le temps aura peut-être tendance à nous séparer. Mais personne ne peut nier qu'ici, derrière les fenêtres de la banlieue de Manchester, survit un amour insensé pour le football, la fête et la musique.

I value truth,

honesty, respect for one another, compassion
and understanding. I have found these
qualities in Manchester United.

I feel close to

the rebelliousness and vigour of the youth
here. Perhaps time will separate us, but
nobody can deny that here, behind the
windows of Manchester, there is an insane
love of football, of celebration and of music.

the technique of
CANTONA

Anyone hoping to emulate the brilliance of Cantona will be sadly disappointed. For his is a God-given talent, and God doesn't give interviews, never mind take evening classes. You will pick up little here in terms of technical instruction, except perhaps a revolutionary approach to the penalty kick. What is on offer though is a purity of intention. This is something which the crudest of cloggers can take out onto the pitch on a Sunday morning — or, if he plays for Wimbledon, on a Saturday afternoon.

Je ne joue pas

contre une équipe en particulier.

Je joue pour me battre contre

l'idée de perdre.

I don't play

against a particular team.
I play to fight against the
idea of losing.

Plus je trouve

que c'est facile, plus ça devient facile.

J'essaie de me persuader que c'est facile.

Et la confiance entraine la liberté, la

liberté de l'expression entraine le

génie, l'euphorie et le feu.

The more I find

it easy, the easier it becomes. I try
to convince myself it's easy. And when
you're confident you find freedom:
from freedom of expression comes
genius, euphoria, and fire.

J'ai connu des joueurs

qui étaient des génies à l'entrainement,
mais qui ne jouaient jamais bien. Le but
de l'entrainement, c'est d'être au mieux
de sa forme les jours de match. C'est le
jeu qui compte.

Ce qui m'interesse

c'est le match qui est à venir.

I've known players

who were geniuses in training but never played well. The point of training is to be at your best on match days. It's the game that counts.

What really interests me

is the next match I have to play.

Je ne connais

qu'une façon de prendre de penalties:

tirer le ballon dans le but.

I know

only one way to take penalties:

to score them.

Il y a toujours

des trucs qu'on aurait pu refaire mieux.
Je marque deux buts. Il est rare que je n'ai
l'occasion de marquer le troisième. Donc
c'est ça le perfectionisme. C'est ce qui te fait
progresser dans la vie.

Whatever happens,

there are always things you could have done better. You score two goals and you usually feel you could have scored a third. That's perfectionism. That's what makes you progress in life.

J'aime à imaginer

que le ballon est vivant, sensible à mon
toucher, à mon pied, à mes caresses, comme
une femme à l'homme qu'elle aime.

I imagine

the ball to be alive, sensitive and responding
to the touch of my foot, to my caresses,
just like a woman with the man she loves.

AT HOME

With the possible exception of an activity which often takes place in the bedroom after Match of the Day on a Saturday, football represents the ultimate union of brain and body, so much so that many footballers remain totally brain-dead in between matches. Not so Eric Cantona. Cantona writes poetry. Cantona paints. He also enjoys the calm of the countryside, a calm broken only by the occasional crack of a shotgun, for - with his famed predatory instincts - Eric Cantona likes to hunt. Bad enough being a goalkeeper - who'd be a pheasant?

Un sportif d'haut niveau

a besoin de trouver son équilibre en dehors
du terrain, de la piste ou des sautoirs.
Personne ne devrait avoir le droit de juger
une telle liberté.

La gloire

coïncide souvent avec la naissance de
relations beaucoup plus superficielles,
fabriquées même.

A top-level sportsman

needs to find his equilibrium outside the
football ground or the running track
or the jumping pits. Nobody has the right
to judge such freedom.

Glory

often coincides with the birth of
superficial relationships.

Un artiste,

à mes yeux, c'est celui qui a le
don d'éclairer une chambre noire.

An artist,

in my eyes, is someone who has
the gift to light up a dark room.

Le silence

de la campagne m'a toujours été
indispensable. Le calme de la nature précède
et suit la fureur des stades. J'ai toujours eu
besoin d'un tel contraste.

Mes tableaux

expriment une foule de rêves, de peurs,
d'angoisse et de pouvoir. Mes poèmes
experiment ma recherche de la liberté.

The silence

of the countryside has always been
indispensable to me. The calm of nature
precedes and follows the storm at the stadium.
I have always needed such a contrast.

My paintings

express many dreams, fears, and much
anguish and power. My poetry is about
the search for freedom.

Je songe

aussi à Marlon Brando, à Mickey Rourke, à tous ces gens fragiles, mais là, debout, bien droits, bien grands, à tous ceux qui t'aident à te trouver, à te retrouver, ou à ne pas te sentir seul dans cette immense société endiablée par le fric.

I think

also of Marlon Brando, of Mickey Rourke,
of all those fragile people who manage
to remain upright, strong and great, of all
those people who help you to find and
refind yourself, and not to feel alone
in this vast world bedevilled by money.

L'important,

c'est d'avoir la force. Je ne sais pas si c'est
l'intelligence - mais la force de trouver une
solution pour ses problèmes.

C'est quand

tu vis des moments difficiles et que
tu t'en sors, tu peux dire, oui, j'ai
d'autre choses, en dehors de mes
talents de footballeur.

The important thing

is to have strength. I don't know if it's
intelligence - but the strength to find a
solution to your problems.

It is when

you hit difficult moments in life, and
you come through, that you can say to
yourself: "Yes, I've other things besides
my footballing talent."

doctor Eric and
MISTER CANTONA

Some would hold that Cantona is a malevolent maverick, a sage of rage, some mutant hybrid of Rimbaud and Rambo, as likely to stud a defender as to pass him, to wallop an official as to accept his decision. The truth is that such reports are wildly exaggerated. During his first two years at Manchester United, Eric Cantona received only three red cards, and one of those was against Arsenal, which hardly counts at all.

Pour atteindre

les sommets de la jouissance, il faut passer par les pires des profondeurs. Le génie, c'est sortir de ce trou dans lequel on s'est mis, ou dans lequel on nous a mis. C'est les échecs qui te font réussir.

Il faut

du talent pour plaire. Je n'ai pas ce talent.

To achieve happiness

you sometimes have to go through the worst depths of despair. Genius is about digging yourself out of the hole you've fallen or been pushed into. Failures make you succeed.

You need

a particular talent to please. I don't have this talent.

Je ne peux pas

voir la passion que j'ai. Un certain feu que tu as en toi et qui demande à sortir et que tu laisse sortir. Quelquefois il a envie de sortir pour faire du mal. Je me fais du mal. Ça me concerne de faire du mal. Ça me concerne de faire du mal aux autres. Mais je ne peux pas être celui que je suis sans ces côtés.

Quand les gens parlent

de toi, c'est que tu existes.
Je suis fier qu'ils parlent de moi.
En bien ou en mal.

I have this passion

in me that I can't handle. It's like a fire
inside you which demands to escape and
which you have to let go. Sometimes it
wants to get out to do harm. I do myself
harm. It worries me when I do harm,
especially to others. But I can't be what I am
without these other sides to my character.

When people talk

about you it's because you exist.
I'm proud that they talk about me.
Whether it's good or bad.

J'ai été renvoyé du terrain

contre St Etienne, et les dirigeants m'ont jugés par rapport à toute ma vie et pas par rapport à un incident isolé. Alors, je leur ai dit qu'ils étaient des idiots, ce qui était une restrainte extraordinaire pour moi.

Il faut que tu fasses

tout pour que ton corps et ton esprit marchent en parallèle. Souvent ils se croisent, donc j'ai souvent à chercher la solution pour qu'ils vivent en accord.

I was sent off

against St Etienne, and the ruling body

passed judgment on my life as

a whole and not just the isolated incident.

So I told them they were idiots,

which was remarkably restrained for me.

You have to

do everything you can to ensure your body

and your mind work in harmony.

In my case, the wires often get crossed, so I

have to find a way to achieve harmony.

Si quelqu'un est different

de l'ordinaire, il est considéré comme fou,

et je suis content d'être considéré comme ça.

Et fier.

Anyone who is different

from the ordinary is considered crazy,

and I am happy to be considered so.

And proud.

J'ai essayé

de me corriger, mais j'a perdu mon jeu.

Quoiqu'on dise,

personne ne me fera changer. Je changerai
quand moi j'ai envie de changer.

Celui qui regrette

se tord la bouche devant la glace au réveil.
Traître aux yeux des autres, il l'est surtout
vis-à-vis de lui-même.

I've tried

to correct myself but I've lost my game.

Whatever people say

no one will make me change.
I'll only change when I want to change.

He who has regrets

grimaces in the mirror when he wakes up in
the morning. He is a traitor to others.
Above all he is betraying himself.

WISDOM

Dennis Wise plays for Chelsea. But wisdom itself is an elusive quality. Sometimes your shots go in; at other times they cannon back off the underside of the bar. That's when they don't uproot the corner flag. And who knows what awaits us when the last referee blows the final whistle. Eric accepts all this, well, philosophically. There will be more goals, that much is certain. But for whom and against whom? Those are the questions.

Alors,

écoute, donne aux autres, prends des

autres, sois toujours toi-même.

Tant mieux encore

si vous chantez parfois en

découvrant mes buts Anglais.

Le reste n'a aucune importance.

Okay,

listen, give to others, take from others, but always be yourself.

So much the better

if my goals give you something to sing about. Nothing else is important.

Quand

on ne sait pas, on a peur.

Le perfectionisme

c'est un besoin. C'est un truc que tu ne peux
pas enseigner. Ou tu en as besoin,
ou tu n'en as pas besoin. C'est une question
de caractère, de ta fierté personnelle.

When

you don't know, you are afraid.

Perfectionism is a need.

It's not something you can teach.
Some people need it, some don't. It's a
question of character, of personal pride.

La vie est toujours

trop cruelle. Tout ce que nous pouvons faire, c'est d'essayer de passer le ballon et de laisser le soleil briller. En espérant qu'il brille sur tout le monde.

Life is always too cruel.
All we can do is say, let's try to
pass the ball and let the sun shine.
Let's just hope it shines on everyone.

We are indebted to the following:

Durrant's Press Agency, the Daily Mail, the Daily Telegraph, the Observer, the Mail on Sunday, Evening Standard, Manchester Evening News, Equipe, Eric Cantona: Un rêve modeste et fou (Robert Laffont), Cantona: My Story (Headline), Standing Room Only (BBC), Ooh Aah Cantona (Pickwick), Eric the King (Man Utd), Alex Griffiths, Nick Leyland, Julian Jordan, Ella Wooltorton and Gorilla Tapes.